## Harvest Creek
### PUBLISHING

Copyright© 2021 by Cindy Masterson

All rights reserved. No portion of this book may be reproduced or transmitted in any form or by any means, electronic or mechanical, including photocopying and recording, or any information storage or retrieval system, except for brief quotations in printed reviews, without written permission from the publisher. Inquiries may be directed to the author.

Editing and cover design by Harvest Creek Design. Illustrations used by permission.

All scripture quotations, unless otherwise indicated, are taken from the New International Version. THE HOLY BIBLE, NEW INTERNATIONAL VERSION®, NIV®, Copyright © 1973, 1978, 1984, 2011 by Biblica, Inc.™ Used by permission. All rights reserved worldwide. The "NIV" and "New International Version" are trademarks registered in the United States Patent and Trademark Office by Biblica, Inc.™

Cindy Masterson
3902 Brighton Drive
Bryan, TX 77802

Our Father, Praying Like Jesus/Cindy Masterson. —1st ed.
ISBN: 978-1-7373567-0-7

Printed in the United States of America

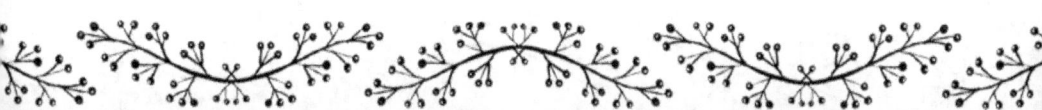

# Dedication

This study is dedicated to my big sister, Carol Neel. She has consistently lived out her Christian faith before me, showing me how to live for Jesus on a daily basis. Her life inspires me!

# Acknowledgments

FIRST, I WANT TO SAY thank you to the Holy Spirit because there would be no study without Him! It was His idea!

Next, I want to thank my friend Teresa Granberry with Harvest Creek Publishing. She has done a fantastic job once again of laying out and editing the study. I am so grateful for her help.

I want to thank two friends, Anne Lowe and Pamela Scheyer, for their help in editing this study. They spent their valuable time going over it, and I greatly appreciate their efforts!

And I also want to thank my husband, Garry Masterson. I have loved serving alongside him for the last 40 years of ministry, and I look forward to many more years of serving together. He truly makes me a better person!

And finally, I want to thank my friends at Celebration Women's Ministry. They have taught me so much over the last 20 years or so about prayer and about serving God, and I love each one of them dearly.

—CINDY MASTERSON

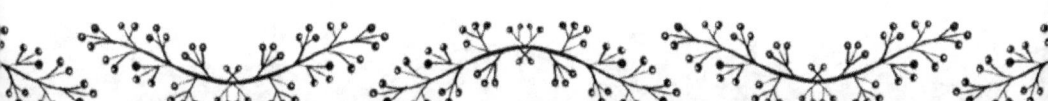

# Foreword

*"I'd love to be closer to God."*
*"I sit down to pray but am not sure how."*
*"I need to pray more."*

MOST OF US WHO CALL OURSELVES CHRISTIANS have thought one or more of these from time to time. We know that prayer is important, essential even, but it often doesn't come easily. Just as we aren't born knowing how to crawl, walk, or run. Christians don't start automatically knowing how to pray.

The good news is that God hasn't left us to wonder. He's offered us a clue sprinkled throughout Scripture, showing us the reasons and patterns of prayer stitched together like a beautifully crafted quilt. We can wrap ourselves in this quilt of prayer and enjoy deep and fulfilling intimacy with the God who created us there. Prayer isn't meant to be simply a duty, a discipline, or a rote practice. It's intended to be a place of knowing and being known, a place where we can rest in God's presence and know that He is listening, caring, and powerful to address and change the things we bring to Him.

We often miss an incredible and surprising fact about prayer: That the God of the universe, Creator of all and Ruler of all, would desire to spend time with us! We wouldn't expect a king or a president to seek one-on-one time with us. And yet here is an authority and power greater than anything on Earth, and He clearly calls us to regularly and intimately spend time in His presence, talking with Him in a tone so intimate that He invites us to call Him "Father."

Even though God is bigger in scope and greater in power than anything our human minds can imagine, He longs to hear our individual needs and joys and to speak life into us.

I'm thankful Cindy Masterson has laid out the Scriptures in this study and given us questions to help us process and discover the beautiful truths there. At some of the most formative times in my life, Cindy has prayed for me. Her deep love for Jesus and her heart for prayer have been influential for me, helping me see that such a prayer life is beautiful and possible.

If you are inspired to pray, longing to know how to pray, and desiring to know our big God at a personal level, these pages will help. They are a trail map guiding us on this journey closer to the heart of God, stopping off at places in the Bible that reveal deep and powerful truth about the God who longs to walk this journey with us as our companion and our guide.

With Joy,
Jessica LaGrone
Dean of Chapel, Asbury Theological Seminary

# How to Use This Study

THIS STUDY WAS CREATED for a weekly format and can be completed through a group of persons or simply by yourself. Each session takes about one hour to complete. You may break each weekly study up into smaller parts for daily use or complete one week all at once.

The sessions utilize the Inductive Bible Study Method, a comprehensive and investigative approach to studying Scripture. Use these three (3) steps in transforming your study of God's word:

- Observe what the text states.
- Interpret what the text means.
- Apply what the text means to and for you.

This study method allows God's Word to explain itself, rather than relying on commentaries and concordances. Use these reference materials only when a concept becomes confusing.

Look for keywords, transitional phrases, key themes, and lists in the Scriptural texts which may offer insight. And most importantly, ask the Holy Spirit to guide your way.

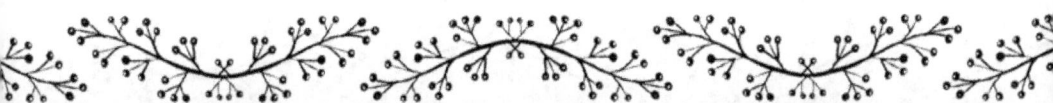

# Weekly Outline

WEEK 1: What is Prayer?..................................17

WEEK 2: Praise and Worship.............................31

WEEK 3: Intercession........................................43

WEEK 4: Supplication and Thanksgiving.........53

WEEK 5: Confession and Protection................63

WEEK 6: Some Final Thoughts on Prayer........75

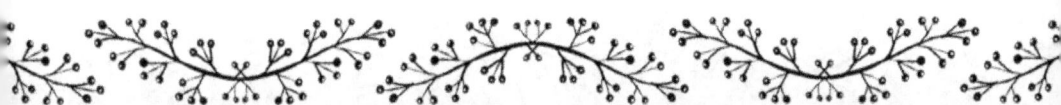

# WEEK 1

# What is Prayer?

> *Remain in me, as I also remain in you. No branch can bear fruit by itself; it must remain in the vine. Neither can you bear fruit unless you remain in me. I am the vine; you are the branches. If you remain in me and I in you, you will bear much fruit; apart from me, you can do nothing.*
> JOHN 15: 4, 5

PRAYER IS SIMPLY, talking to God, calling on His name. To a Christian, prayer is as essential as breathing. It is the way we stay connected to the vine. (John 15:4, 5)

Why does Jesus say it's essential to stay connected?

Let's look at some passages that address what prayer is. Read Genesis 4:26. As the population of the Earth grew in number, what did the people begin to do?

The book of Psalms is a collection of poems often used as songs or devotions to the Lord. But they also provided instruction to the people of God. Let's look at some passages from the Psalms, which are considered the Israelites prayer book.

In Psalm 4, David begins with a short prayer. What does he ask God to do in Psalm 4:1?

What does David do in Psalm 17:6, and why?

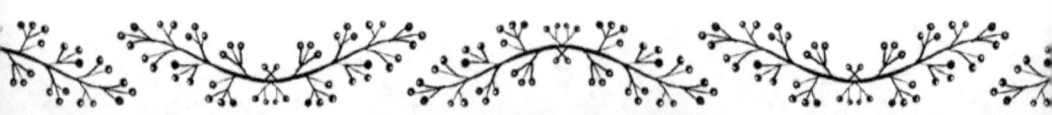

What three instructions does God give Israel in Psalm 50:14,15? And what will He do as a result of following those instructions?

   1.

   2.

   3.

Read Psalm 86:3-7. What does David say that he does in verse 3? In verse 5, what does he say about those who call on God?

In Psalm 116:1,2, what does the Psalmist say he will do and why?

According to Psalm 145:18-19, what does God do?

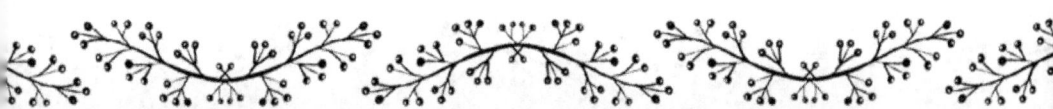

The prophet Isaiah wrote one of the most beautiful books in the Bible. What does he say to do in Isaiah 55:6?

Now let's look at the New Testament. What does Paul say in Romans 10:12,13 about those who call upon the Lord?

> *Jesus answered, "I am the way and the truth and the life. No one comes to the Father except through me.*
> *JOHN 14:6*

According to the passage above, how do we come to the Father?

Hebrews 10:19-22 describes the process we use to draw near to God. Restate this passage in your own words.

We can just call on the name of the Lord, and He will hear us, and we will be saved. We need to know and trust Jesus to be heard by God. *If you aren't sure about this in your life, reference the Celebration Women's Ministry study on Salvation, available from www.celebrationministries.org.*

## So why should we pray?

One reason is that God tells us to do so. Also, Jesus felt the need to regularly pray. And if Jesus needed to pray, then surely, we need to, as well!

A good verse on prayer and why to pray is Jeremiah 33:2-3. I especially like how The Message puts it. The Creator God who made the universe is willing to tell us things we could never know or figure out on our own unless we pray.

> *Continue earnestly in prayer, being vigilant in it with thanksgiving.*
> COLOSSIANS 4:2

What does it mean to be "earnest" in prayer?




What does it mean to be "vigilant" in prayer?




I Thessalonians 5:16-18 gives three directives for the brethren:

1. _____ always.

2. _____ without ceasing.

3. _____ _____ give thanks.


What does Paul want the men and women of the church to do in I Timothy 2:8?

James was one of the leaders in the early church. It is also believed that he was Jesus' half-brother. In times of trouble, what does James 5:13 say to do?




Why does 1 Peter 4:7 say we are to be alert and sober-minded?




In Matthew 6:5, Jesus doesn't say "*if* you pray," but instead, he says, "*when* you pray." What does this imply?




Read Matthew 14:23 and Mark 6:46. What do these verses teach that Jesus did after he had been with the multitudes?

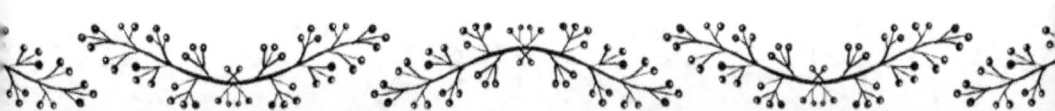

In Luke 6:12, 13, what does Jesus do after he prays all night? What kind of decision does he make?

Describe what happens in Luke 9:28-32. What happens then?

Read Luke 11:1-4. What do the disciples ask Jesus to do?

What was Peter doing in Acts 10:9?

We can see that prayer is important! When and where did Jesus and Peter pray? What does this mean for you and me? Do you have a specific time set aside to pray, as well?

As you have learned, Jesus had a regular custom of praying. And this did not go unnoticed by his disciples. There was something about observing Jesus pray that stirred a hunger within his followers.

One day, one of the disciples asked Jesus to teach them more about how to pray. In Luke 11:1-4, Jesus provides specific training on prayer to his disciples. Let's look at what the scriptures have to say about how we pray.

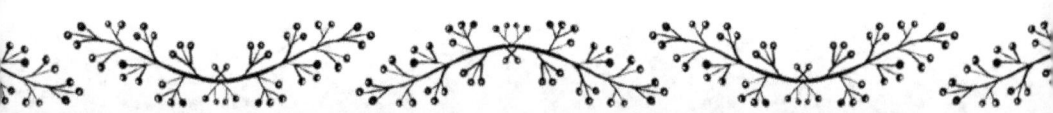

> *He said to them, "When you pray, say:*
> *"'Father, hallowed be your name,*
> *your kingdom come. Give us each day our*
> *daily bread. Forgive us our sins,*
> *for we also forgive everyone who sins*
> *against us. And lead us not into*
> *temptation."*
> LUKE 11: 2-4

# Our Father

Matthew 6:9-13 features this same prayer—a model prayer that Jesus gave his disciples. This passage has become what most Christians now refer to as "the Lord's Prayer." It wasn't necessarily meant to be repeated but used as a guide to formulate your own prayers.

The New Living Translation expresses this model prayer beautifully and will be used throughout our discussion of the Lord's Prayer.

How does the prayer begin? It starts with "Our Father." It doesn't start with "my Father," but ours. We are family, and we need to bear that in mind as we pray.

What does John 1:12 say about who we are, if we receive him and believe in his name?




According to Romans 8:14-17. Who does Paul say we are if we are led by the Spirit? What can we cry out to God?




In Galatians 4, verses 4-7, we learn more about why God sent his son. What does God say about what he has done? How does this passage relate to beginning prayer with "Our Father?"




"Abba" is a term of endearment, like Daddy. So, in referring to God as our Abba Father, we indicate a high level of intimacy. We can and should call on the name of God our Father, our Daddy.

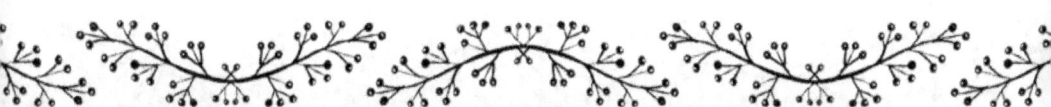

# In Heaven

Matthew 6:9 tells us where our Father resides. Where does Hebrews 8:1, 2 say that Jesus is right now? Also, in Hebrews 1:3?

Where does 1 Peter 3:22 say that Jesus is now?

And where is our citizenship, according to Philippians 3:20?

The Bible teaches that Heaven is where God dwells, along with His angels and redeemed children. Where is Heaven? We don't know, but we know that God is there.

And Jesus is present with God in Heaven. Since God and Jesus are "omnipresent" through the Holy Spirit, they can be in Heaven *and* with us, as well.

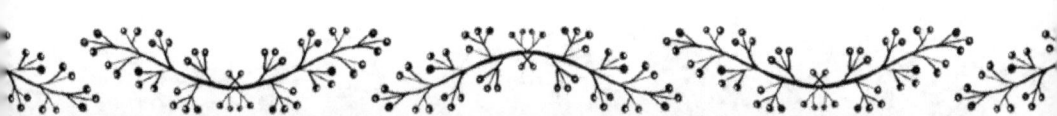

# What Have I Learned This Week?

Reflect on the thoughts you have gained during this week's Bible study:

_____
_____
_____
_____
_____
_____
_____
_____
_____
_____
_____
_____
_____

What can now be applied to your daily walk with the Lord:

_____
_____
_____
_____
_____
_____
_____
_____

# WEEK 2

# Praise and Worship

> *This, then, is how you should pray:*
> *"Our Father in Heaven,*
> *hallowed be your name*
> *MATTHEW 6:9*

## May Your Name Be Kept Holy

AFTER HE TEACHES US to say, "Our Father, who is in Heaven," then He says, "Holy be your name." He praises God. We should always begin our prayers with praise and worship.

We often use these words together, as in "praise and worship time," but are they the same thing? Let's look at what Scripture says about this.

Most often translated as "worship" in the Old and New Testaments, both the Hebrew and Greek words have to do with bowing down, prostrating oneself before God.

The Hebrew words translated as "praise" have to do with thanksgiving, singing praise, or honoring someone. Praise comes out of a heart of worship. The people of that day would frequently stand to praise!

# Worship

What does II Chronicles 20:18 say that the Jehoshaphat and the people of Judah did as they worshiped God?

King Hezekiah was a reformer king who did right in the eyes of the Lord. What did the King and all of Israel do in II Chronicles 29:28,29?

What does Psalm 95:6 call on us to do?

Job was a man who suffered greatly. During tremendous loss and affliction, he continues on with his confession of faith in God. What does Job do in Job 1:20 after his significant losses?

What did the twenty-four elders do in Revelation 5:8 & 14?

What do the above passages tell us about our posture before God as we worship Him? What does this have to do with our heart attitudes?

What kind of worshippers is God looking for, based on Jesus' words in John 4:23,24?

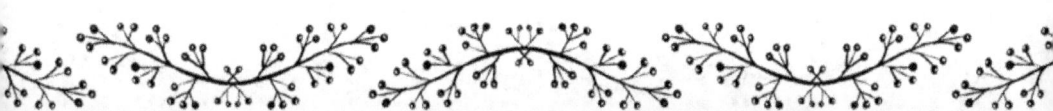

According to Romans 12:1, what is true and proper worship?




God is looking for those who will worship in Spirit and Trust and with their whole hearts. We can see that often, in the Bible, people would bow down to worship. What did they do to praise Him? Let's look and see.



# Praise

Read I Chronicles 23:28-30. What were the duties of the Levites? What were the Levites to do when they thanked and praised the Lord?

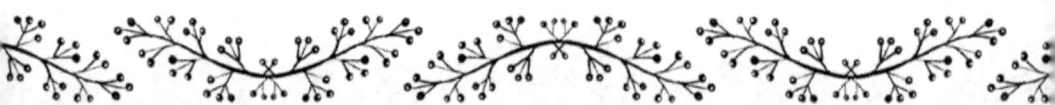

Look at II Chronicles 20:19; what tone did the Levites use here when they stood and praised the Lord?

What did the Levites tell the people to do in Nehemiah 9:5,6? Read the entire chapter to get a better feel for what was happening here.

We can see that people often stood up to praise God! They were what I call "full-body worshipers." They were even pretty loud sometimes! Sometimes they bowed down, sometimes they stood up. Sometimes they raised their hands (Read Psalms 28:2, 134:2, 141:2, 143:6, and I Timothy 2:8), and sometimes they danced (Read Exodus 15:20, Jeremiah 31:4, II Samuel 6:14-16, Psalms 30:11, 149:3, and 150:4). How does this compare to Sunday morning worship for most of us?

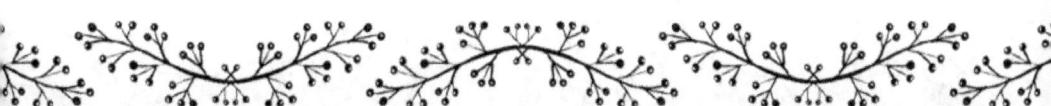

# Why Should We Praise God?

 What does Psalm 145 teach about why we praise God? List the reasons.

What does Psalm 148 say about *who* should praise God and *why*?

One of my favorite scriptures, which refers to praise, is II Chronicles 20:21-23. In this passage, King Jehoshaphat has inquired of the Lord about a particular battle, and the Lord has told him that the battle is His (the Lord's). God is literally saying that He is going to fight the battle for the King.

So, as you read this passage for yourself, look at what Jehoshaphat does. Comment below on what the king does.

I love that they sent the people praising out in the front of the battle. This is how we are to fight our battles—praising Him!

The people were singing their praises. This is something that often happens in Scripture.

## Singing Praise

Deborah was an Old Testament prophetess and one of the only female judges of Israel. She was known for her wisdom and courage as a military strategist. Deborah instructed her protégé, Barak, to take 10,000 troops to Mount Tabor and confront an army general named Sisera.

Barak didn't want to go unless Deborah went with him. So, she agreed to go into battle with the troops. But she cautioned that there will be no glory for Barak if she went

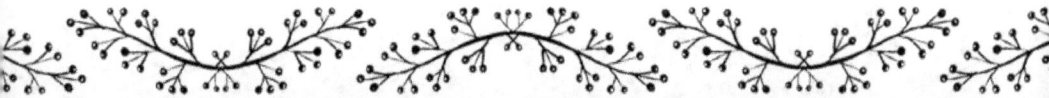

along because the Lord would be delivering Sisera into the hands of a woman.

Judges 5:1-3, known as the "Song of Deborah," is a passage where she exults her victory over Sisera's army. What does Deborah say that she will do in these verses?




Like Deborah, during the reign of David, he faced numerous battles against the Philistines. Each time, the opponent fell at the hands of David and his men.

II Samuel 22:1 describes what David did when the Lord delivered him from his enemies.

As David grew in years, he began gathering the leaders of Israel in preparation to transition his reign to his son, Solomon. He appointed people to various tasks, including overseeing the temple building and serving as judges and officials within the Kingdom.

In addition to the assignment of royal gatekeepers, how many people did David appoint to praise God with musical instruments, according to I Chronicles 23:5?

What did David instruct us to do in Psalm 95:1,2?

The final Psalm is the 150th which urges people to use music and dancing to praise God. What eight instruments are mentioned in Psalm 150?

1.
2.
3.
4.
5.
6.
7.
8.

What were the twenty-four elders and the four living creatures doing in Revelation 5: 8, 9?

Sometimes offering praise and worship is difficult, especially in the middle of difficult circumstances, but this is precisely when we need to praise Him. Hebrews 13:15 speaks of bringing a sacrifice of praise. To me, this refers to praising even when it's hard to do so!

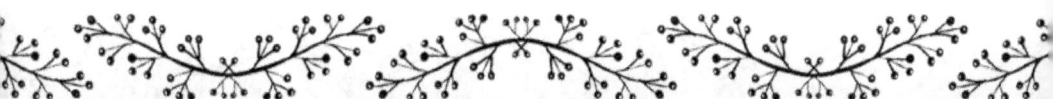

Have you ever praised God during a difficult circumstance? What happened?

What does David say in Psalm 30:11,12 about what God will do for him amid praise?

Praise invites God's power into our lives. Let's look at Paul and Silas in Acts 16:23-26. What was their situation, and what were they doing in the middle of it? What was God's response?

When should we praise the Lord? All the time—during both difficult times and good times. How can we praise Him? The Psalms are an excellent way to praise the Lord. You can use them to "prime the pump," so to speak. Psalms 145 through 150 are particularly good passages to pray.

Another helpful idea is to pray the alphabet, go letter-by-letter, and praise the Lord for things about Him that begin with each letter. For example, God, you are **A**wesome, **B**eautiful, **C**reative, etc. You can use this type of praise at anytime, anywhere, without having a Bible on hand.

It is always good to begin time with the Lord in worship and praise!

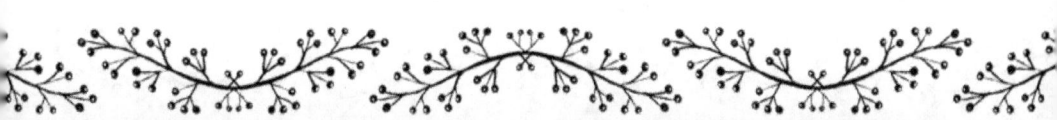

# What Have I Learned This Week?

Reflect on the thoughts you have gained during this week's Bible study:

_____
_____
_____
_____
_____
_____
_____
_____
_____
_____
_____
_____
_____
_____

What can now be applied to your daily walk with the Lord:

_____
_____
_____
_____
_____
_____
_____
_____

# WEEK 3

# Intercession

> *May your Kingdom come soon. May your will be done on Earth as it is in Heaven.*
> MATTHEW 6:10

THE NEXT PART OF THE PRAYER that Jesus teaches pertains to praying for God's Kingdom to come.
I believe this refers to intercession for others for God's will to be done in their lives and ours. So, after we praise and worship God, then we can begin to ask him for things.

What does it mean to intercede? It means to go before someone on behalf of someone else, making requests.

Read the following passages: Romans 8:34 and Hebrews 7:23-25. What do these passages say about who intercedes for us?

What does the prophet say to do in Lamentations 2:19? Who does he tell them to pray for?




What does Paul urge us to do in I Timothy 2:1-4? Who does he instruct us to intercede for, and why?




What does Jesus say in Luke 18:1-7 say about giving up in prayer?




Read Acts 12:5-16. Peter had been put in jail by King Herod. What does verse 5 say that the church was doing for Peter? Were they surprised by the answer in verses 15 and 16? Should we be surprised when God answers our prayers?

How do we intercede for people? What should we pray? Let's look at some examples of this in the Scriptures.

Who does Jesus tell us to pray for in Matthew 5:44-45, and why?

What does Jesus tell us to do for enemies in Luke 6:27, 28? Is this easy to do?

What does Jesus pray for us in John 17:20,21? Why does he pray this?

In the course of his imprisonment, Paul appeared before King Agrippa II and stated his case. What does Paul pray in Acts 26:29?

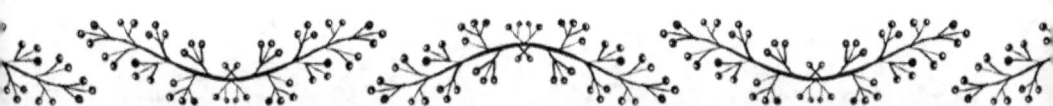

What does Paul say that he does for the church at Ephesus? What does he pray for them in Ephesians 1: 15-21?




What else does Paul pray for them in Ephesians 3:14-21?




In Philippians 1:3-6, what does Paul say about how he prays for this group of people? What does he pray in verses 9-11?




What does Paul say about what he does for the church in Colossae, in Colossians 1:3,9-12?

Who does Paul ask them to pray for him in Colossians 4:3,4?

What does James tell us to do in James 5:13-18? Who does he compare us to?

As read in the passage above, when we pray for each other and confess our sins to one another, WE are healed. Interceding for others heals us, too.

In Hebrews 13:18-19, what does the writer ask them to do for him?

How does John pray for his friend in III John 1:2?

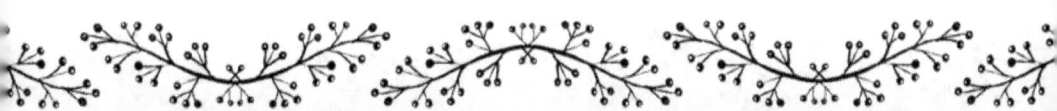

What does Paul pray for the church in Thessalonica in I Thessalonians 3:10-13?




What does Paul pray for in II Thessalonians 1:11,12?




What does he ask them to pray for him in II Thessalonians 3:1,2?




What does John say in I John 5:14-15 say about praying for the will of God?

How can we know what the will of God is? We can look at the Scripture for one thing. Also, look at the Word made flesh—Jesus!

One way that we can pray the will of God is by praying the Scriptures. Some of the passages we looked at earlier today make excellent prayers to pray for other people. You can also take a scripture passage and convert it into a prayer.

For example, from Psalm 23, the Lord is my shepherd could be, "Lord be my child's shepherd today; make them aware of your presence in their lives."

Another example is Psalm 51. *"Have mercy on my children, O God, according to your unfailing love; according to your great compassion, blot out their transgressions."*

Simply personalize the Scriptures. Of course, we depend on the Holy Spirit to guide our prayers, and we also want to look at the context of the Scriptures that we are going to use.
Take a Scripture and write a prayer for someone you know.

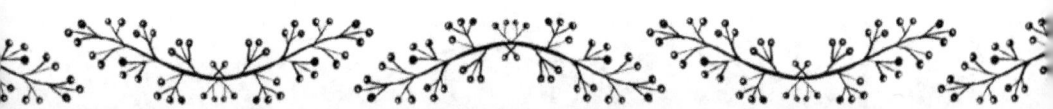

There are several excellent resources for praying the Scripture. Celebration Women's Ministry has an excellent booklet called Praying the Scriptures-The Power of Praying God's Word on their website at:

www.celebrationministries.org

Also, the **Echo Prayer App** is a great way to keep track of your prayer requests for others. I have this app set to remind me to pray for my grandchildren all throughout the day!

# What Have I Learned This Week?

Reflect on the thoughts you have gained during this week's Bible study:

_____
_____
_____
_____
_____
_____
_____
_____
_____
_____
_____
_____
_____
_____

What can now be applied to your daily walk with the Lord:

_____
_____
_____
_____
_____
_____
_____

# WEEK 4

# Supplication &

# Thanksgiving

> *"Give us today the bread we need."*
> MATTHEW 6:11

AFTER INTERCEDING AND PRAYING FOR OTHERS, we should also pray for our *own* needs.
The Bible refers to this form of prayer as supplication, a call for help from God.

Supplication means earnestly and humbly asking for something.

What does Jesus say about humility in prayer in Luke 18: 10-14?

In that same passage, which man went home having had his prayer heard?

What does David say he does in Psalm 5:1-3?

What does Jesus say we are to do in Matthew 7:7-11, and what will God do?

Read Luke 11:5-8. What does this passage say about praying?

In Luke 21, Jesus seems to be speaking about the end times. What does Jesus say in Luke 21:36 that we are to pray for?

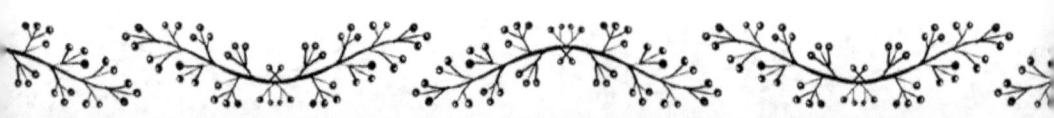

Read John 14:14-17. What does Jesus say about how we are to pray? What will he give those who ask?

Read Chapter 15 of John. According to verses 7 and 8, what can we do if we remain in Him?

What does He say we should do in John 16:23-27?

Read Mark 11:23,24. What does this passage say about prayer?

What does Jesus say in Matthew 18:19-20 say about when we pray together?

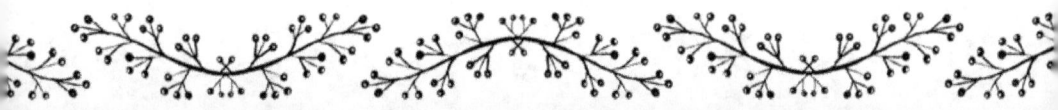

The early church was persecuted and told to stop speaking about Jesus, so what did they pray for in Acts 4:24-30? And what happened in verse 31?

In Romans 1:10-12, what does Paul pray for himself?

What does he ask them to pray in Romans 15:30-32?

What does Paul tell us to do in Philippians 4:6,7?

This is a beautiful passage on prayer. In it, Paul says not to worry about anything, but instead to pray about everything, making your requests known to God, and He will give you peace. What a tremendous promise! Instead of worrying, try praying and giving thanks!

Read I Thessalonians 3:9-11. What does Paul pray for himself in verse 10? What does he ask them to pray for him in verse 11? What does he ask them to do in I Thessalonians 5:25?

What does James 5:13-15 say we are to do if we are suffering or sick?

So, there is nothing wrong with asking God for help in the situations in our own life. Once again, we need to pray according to God's will, but his promises are sure.

In much the same way we love and care for our own children, God loves and cares for us. Although His love and care are far greater than ours! You will notice that most of Paul's prayers were for his ministry, not his own body. Although we do know that he prayed for himself. Look at II Corinthians 12:8. How many times did he ask God to take away his thorn in the flesh?

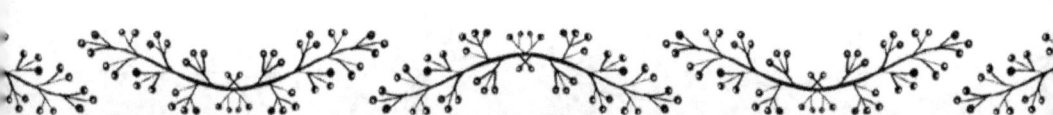

# Thanksgiving

Often, our prayers and petitions are combined with thanksgiving. This is an element of prayer that shows faith. If we pray with thanksgiving, we are giving God the glory for the work He's already done, or we are thanking God in advance for what he is going to do.

What does David say in I Chronicles 29:13?




According to Nehemiah 12:27, what kinds of songs did the Levites sing at the dedication of the wall of Jerusalem?




How does David say he will praise God's name in Psalm 69:30?

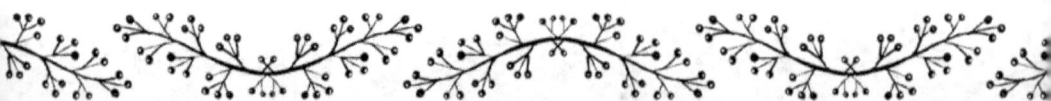

How does the Psalmist say we should come to the Lord in verses 1 & 2 of Psalm 95?

How does Psalm 100:4 say we are to enter God's gates? What does this mean for us today?

How does Paul pray in I Thessalonians 1:2?

How does Paul tell Timothy to pray in I Timothy 2:1?

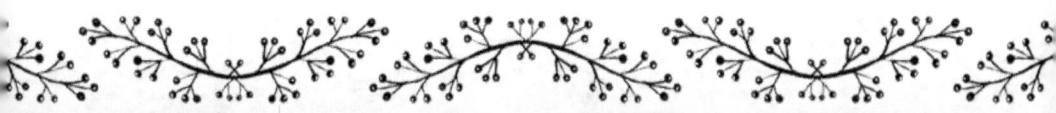

What does Paul say about our speech in Ephesians 5:4?




What does Paul say in Colossians 3:15 that we are to do?
What does he say to do in Colossians 4:2?




What does Hebrews 12:28,29 say we are to do?




What does Philemon 1:4,5 say about how Paul prays for them?

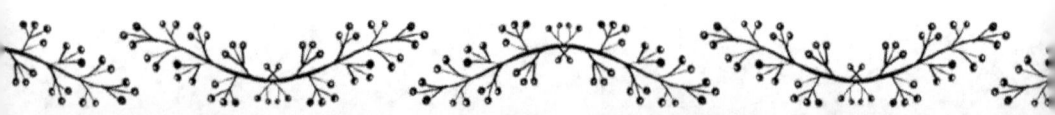

So, as we pray for ourselves (and others), thanksgiving is important. You might even say we should have a thankful attitude or an "attitude of gratitude."

What can you do to cultivate that attitude this week? Perhaps start a "Thankfulness" journal. Begin each page by expressing appreciation for what you have in your life right now. List the person(s) you are grateful for and the good things available to you at this moment.

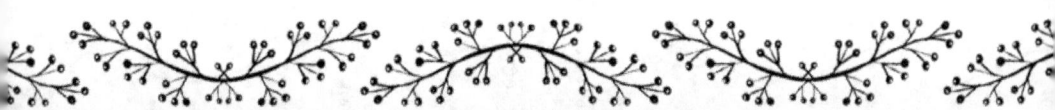

# What Have I Learned This Week?

Reflect on the thoughts you have gained during this week's Bible study:

_____
_____
_____
_____
_____
_____
_____
_____
_____
_____
_____
_____
_____

What can now be applied to your daily walk with the Lord:

_____
_____
_____
_____
_____
_____
_____

# WEEK 5

# Confession and Protection

> "Forgive us our sins, as we have forgiven those who sin against us."
> MATTHEW 6:12

THE NEXT THING JESUS TALKS ABOUT is forgiveness of sins. This is very important in prayer!

Read Psalm 32:1-5. In verses 1 and 2, who does David say is blessed? What does he say happened to him in verses 3&4? And then what happens in verse 5?

What does David say in Psalm 51 about his sin with Bathsheba? (*Read II Samuel 11 for the entire story*). David was caught and called out by the prophet Samuel. What does he say about himself in verses 3-5 of Psalm 51? In verse 17, what kind of sacrifice does he say that God wants from him?

What is Daniel doing in chapter 9:20,21? This is in the midst of a prayer for his people.

What does II Chronicles 7:14 say that the people of God need to do before He will come and heal their land?

Read Nehemiah 9:1-3. What did the Israelites do here? If you read the chapter before, you can see that they were in the middle of celebrating one of the feasts.

In the Old Covenant, there were rituals for dealing with our sins. All the ritual sacrifices are detailed in Leviticus. In the New Covenant, there is Jesus!

Where does Jesus say that forgiveness comes from in Matthew 26:27,28?

What did Jesus say about forgiveness in Luke 24:46,47?

Where does Peter say that forgiveness comes from in Acts 10:34-43? This is Peter's speech to the Gentiles gathered in Cornelius' house. At the end of his speech, where does Peter say that forgiveness comes from?

According to Paul in Ephesians 1:7, where does forgiveness come from?


The book of Hebrews speaks to the New Covenant. Read Hebrews 9:22-26. What does this say that Jesus has done for us?


We have forgiveness through the shed blood of Jesus. Thank you, Jesus, for shedding your blood for our forgiveness! How important is it in the New Testament to forgive others? Let's look at what Jesus says in Mark 11:25. What does Jesus tell them to do while they are praying and why?


What does Jesus say about forgiveness in Matthew 6:14,15?

Peter was always looking for an angle, it seemed. What does he ask Jesus in Matthew 18: 21? How does Jesus answer him in verse 22? Read the rest of the chapter. What does Jesus say about forgiveness in the story that follows?

What does Jesus tell us to do in Luke 6:36,37?

What does Paul say in Colossians 3:13 about what we are to do?

What does James 2:12,13 say about how we are to speak and act?

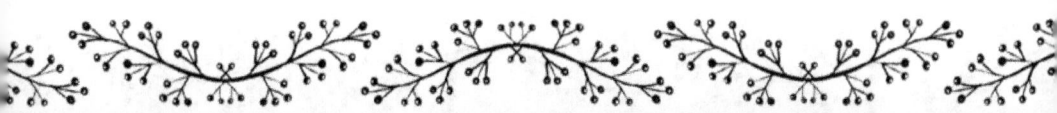

We have been forgiven so much; how can we withhold forgiveness from someone whom God has forgiven? Unforgiveness can block our prayers, as well as any unconfessed sin.

What does 1 John 1:8-10 say we are to do when we sin? What will Jesus do for us? What does 2:1,2 say about when we sin?

What does James 5:16 say about what we are to do with our sins?

Consider what this means in your life. Do you have someone you need to forgive? Do you have someone in your life that you trust enough to share with? Sometimes things need to be brought out into the light for healing to take place.

# Protection

After he talks about forgiveness, he then says:

> *"And don't let us yield to temptation, but rescue us from the evil one."*
> MATTHEW 6:13

He is talking about keeping us safe.

Psalm 91 is a song of protection. Read the whole Psalm. What does David say that God will do for him in verses 14-16? Go on to read Psalm 121 for more insight.

What does Jesus say about why the disciples should pray in Luke 22:40 & 46? (This is also taught in Matthew 26:41 and Mark 14:38) What was going on around these verses?

What does Paul say about temptation in I Corinthians 10:13?




What is Jesus' prayer for us in John 17:15?




Paul had enemies everywhere he went. He had undoubtedly run across many unreasonable men in his day. What does Paul ask the church in Thessalonica to pray for him in II Thessalonians 3:2? What does he say that the Lord will do for them? (vs. 3)




What does Peter say in I Peter 5:8,9 about our enemy? What are we to do?

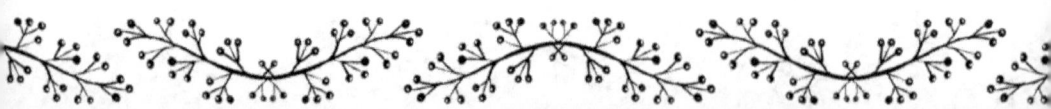

What does James 4:7 say we are to do?

Our part is to pray, resist the enemy and draw near to God. God's part is to protect us from the evil one.

How does Jesus end the model prayer? With praise!

> *"For yours is the Kingdom and the power and the glory forever."*
> MATTHEW 6:13

We ended up right back where we started, with praise and worship. Amen, which means "so be it!"

# Authority

We often end our prayers by saying, "In Jesus' name, Amen." Why do we do that? Well, the Scripture instructs us to do this. Read John 14:14. What does this say about how to pray?

What does Jesus say in John 16:23-27?




What does it mean to pray "In Jesus' name?" I believe it means to pray with the authority that Jesus gives us. If we come in someone else's name who has authority, then we, too, have that authority.

Read Matthew 8:8,9. What did the Centurion soldier understand about Jesus?




What did Jesus give his disciples in Matthew 10:1? What did he send them out to do?




What did Jesus say in Matthew 28:18?

What does it mean to pray with authority? I believe it means to pray like Peter did in Acts 3:6. Read that verse below:

> *Then Peter said, "Silver or gold I do not have, but what I do have I give you. In the name of Jesus Christ of Nazareth, walk."*

Think about what Peter told the man. Did he say, "Lord, heal this man?" No, he spoke with authority in the name of Jesus Christ and told the man to be healed. Sometimes God calls us to pray in this way.

# What Have I Learned This Week?

Reflect on the thoughts you have gained during this week's Bible study:

_____
_____
_____
_____
_____
_____
_____
_____
_____
_____
_____
_____
_____

What can now be applied to your daily walk with the Lord:

_____
_____
_____
_____
_____
_____
_____

# WEEK 6

# Some Final Thoughts on Prayer

JESUS GAVE US the model prayer, but he also had some other teachings on prayer. Let's look at some of these.

## Prayer and Fasting

Prayer and fasting are often mentioned together in Scripture. We are referring to fasting as giving up something for the purpose of prayer. Usually, this relates to food, but it could be other things such as a social media fast.

What does Jehoshaphat do in II Chronicles 20:3? Why does he do this, according to verse 2?




What does Ezra do in Ezra 8:21? Why does he do this? They were preparing to return from the Exile.




What did the Israelites do in Nehemiah 9:1,2?




Read Esther 4:4-17. What does Queen Esther tell Mordechai to do in Verse 16? Esther was preparing to go see the King. What could have happened to Esther?

What did the Ninevites do in response to Jonah's preaching? Read Jonah 3:5.




Daniel has just heard from the Lord that the desolation of Israel would last 70 years. What does Daniel do in chapter 9, verses 1-6?




What does God say about how they fasted in Isaiah 58:1-11? What about Zechariah 7:1-10?




Fasting alone isn't enough. Our lives and hearts have to be right as well. What does Jesus say about this in Matthew 6:16-18? Does he say "*if*" you fast or "*when*" you fast? What does this imply?

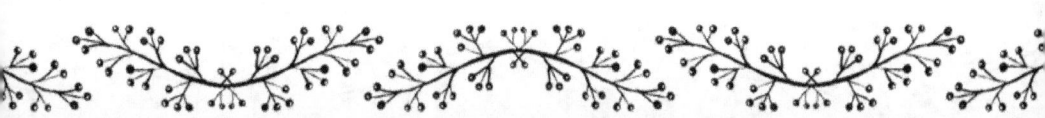

What did Jesus do before he was tempted by the devil, according to Matthew 4:2?




What was the church doing when the Holy Spirit spoke to them, according to Acts 13:2?




Read Acts 14:23. How did Paul and Barnabas appoint elders in the churches?




Fasting is done in response to significant issues and before big decisions. It is also an excellent spiritual discipline. Have you ever tried fasting? What did you do? Describe your experience.

# Praying in the Spirit

Read Ephesians 6:13-17. Paul directs us to put on the full armor of God to battle the spiritual forces. Who does he say that we are battling?

After Paul tells us to put on the whole armor of God, what does he ask us to do in Ephesians 6:18?

What do we read in Romans 8:26,27 about praying in the Spirit?

Some people believe that praying in the Spirit means praying in a prayer language or praying in tongues. What does Paul say about speaking in tongues in I Corinthians 12:10? Do some people have this gift? Does everybody have it?

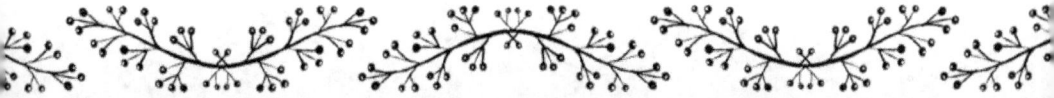

Paul teaches much about praying in the Spirit in the fourteenth chapter of I Corinthians. What does he say about it in I Corinthians 14:2, 13-15, and 18-19?

How does Jude tell us to pray in verses 20,21?

We are told to pray in the Spirit. What does that look like for you?

I believe it means being open to the move of the Spirit and asking for His help as we pray.

# When God Doesn't Answer

What do we do when God doesn't answer the way we want him to? Sometimes we pray according to God's will, as we understand it. We stand in faith believing, and we still don't get the answer we want. What do we do then?

Well, we can either stop praying, or we can look at what God says about this in His word. We know that we don't understand fully now (I Corinthians 13:12), but we will know fully when we see Him face-to-face. There are circumstances that we will only know when we meet Jesus face to face.

How does Jesus refer to this problem in Mark 6:4-6?




Where does Ephesians 2:8 say that faith comes from?

Read Matthew 17:15-20. What did Jesus say the problem was in verse 20? Does it take a lot of faith?

Sometimes our lack of faith causes our prayers to go unanswered. But is it always a lack of faith? No, I don't believe so.

Read II Samuel 12:15-23. David was a man after God's own heart. What does he do when his son becomes ill? How does David respond when his son dies in verse 20?

Let's look at the life of Paul. Paul was an amazing man of God who wrote most of the New Testament, yet he struggled. We don't know exactly what his struggle was, but we know that he didn't receive the answer he hoped for.

What does II Corinthians 12:7-10 say about Paul's experience? What did he pray for? And what was God's answer?

What does Paul do in verse 10?

When we are weak, he is strong in us! Therefore, we are strong in him!

What does the writer of Habakkuk 3:17-19 say he will do when things don't go his way?

Read Mark 9:21-27. What does the Father ask of Jesus in verse 24? May we cry out with the same prayer: Lord, help our unbelief!

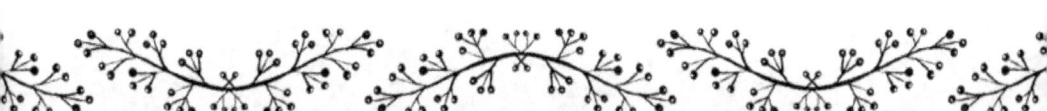

# In Summary

We can pray the way that Jesus taught us to, following the model of the Lord's prayer. We can pray with the authority of Jesus' name. We can also fast and pray. And we can pray in the Spirit.

All of these things are essential in prayer. We can stand in faith, believing God will answer because He says He will. However, when He doesn't answer the way we think He should, we can trust Him because He is good and trustworthy. Thank you, Father, for the gift of prayer.

> *"Now to him who is able to do immeasurably more than all we ask or imagine, according to his power that is at work within us, to him be glory in the church and in Christ Jesus throughout all generations, forever and ever! Amen."*
> EPHESIANS 3:20,21

# What Have I Learned This Week?

Reflect on the thoughts you have gained during this week's Bible study:

_____
_____
_____
_____
_____
_____
_____
_____
_____
_____
_____
_____
_____
_____

What can now be applied to your daily walk with the Lord:

_____
_____
_____
_____
_____
_____
_____

# Endorsements

In 2012, I was blessed to participate in a ladies' Bible study where I became friends with our teacher Cindy Masterson. Cindy had a real passion for the Word and taught how Scripture is used to help us through our everyday lives. She taught us how important it was to have a personal relationship with Christ and with our sisters in Christ. We learned from her the power of prayer and how God longs to hear from us each and every day, not just when times are tough. Her boldness in Christ and her sense of humor led me to understand my need for a closer relationship with my Savior and His amazing desire to know me. I am positive that you will also be blessed by Cindy's teachings.

**Stormy King, Woodcrest United Methodist Church**
**Lumberton, TX**

My life has been profoundly impacted by Cindy Masterson. She discipled me in my early twenties as a newlywed and new mom. Her heart for Jesus was contagious, and I knew I wanted what she had, a deep and abiding relationship with the Lord. She taught me to seek God wholeheartedly and to lead others to do the same. I will be forever grateful for the years that Cindy discipled me!

**Abby Muirhead, Northside Christian Church**
**Spring, TX**

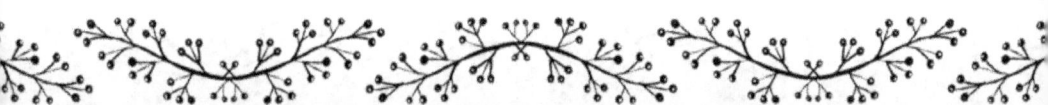

Cindy Masterson is a gifted Bible study teacher. May God's Word about prayer encourage you in your prayer life.

**Judy C. Graham, President, and Co-Founder, Celebration Women's Ministry, Inc.**

I have known Cindy for twenty years and witnessed her passion for sharing God's Word with women. She knows the Word and believes it is transforming. More importantly, she knows God. She knows what it means to abide in Him. Cindy is not only an anointed teacher but a prayer warrior—a woman of deep, unshakeable faith and abiding prayer.

Thank you, Cindy, for teaching us what God's Word says about prayer and giving us the confidence to pray with faith and belief. I was encouraged and blessed by this study on prayer, and I know you will be as well.

**Pamela Fulbright-Scheyer, Celebration Women's Ministry - National Prayer Team**

# About the Author

CINDY MASTERSON loves teaching women about the truth in God's word. Whether through a small group at her local church or as a guest speaker for a national women's ministry, you will always find her sharing her knowledge of the Bible. She believes it contains everything one needs to become equipped to share the good news to a lost world.

As a part of Celebration Women's Ministry (an outreach of the United Methodist Church), women across America have participated in three different bible studies written by Cindy.

www.ingramcontent.com/pod-product-compliance
Lightning Source LLC
LaVergne TN
LVHW051151080426
835508LV00021B/2587